# 60-DAY
# HOLY SPIRIT
# DEVOTIONAL

# 60-DAY
# HOLY SPIRIT
# DEVOTIONAL

DR. KEVIN L. ZADAI

Cover design: Virtually Possible Designs

For more information about our school, go to www.warriornotesschool.com. Reach us on the internet: www.Kevinzadai.com
ISBN 13 TP: 978-1-6631-0017-7

# Dedication

I dedicate this book to the Lord Jesus Christ. When I died during surgery and met with Jesus on the other side, He insisted that I return to life on the earth and that I help people with their destinies. Because of Jesus' love and concern for people, the Lord has actually chosen to send a person back from death to help everyone who will receive that help so that his or her destiny and purpose are secure in Him. I want You, Lord, to know that when You come to take me to be with You someday, it is my sincere hope that people remember not me, but the revelation of Jesus Christ that You have revealed through me. I want others to know that I am merely being obedient to Your Heavenly calling and mission, which is to reveal Your plan for the fulfillment of the divine destiny for each of God's children.

# Acknowledgments

In addition to sharing my story with everyone through the book *Heavenly Visitation: A Guide to the Supernatural,* I have been commissioned by God to write over 50 books and study guides. Most recently, the Lord gave me the commission to produce this *60-Day Holy Spirit Devotional.* This daily devotional addresses some of the revelations concerning the areas that Jesus reviewed and revealed to me through the Word of God and by the Spirit of God during several visitations. I want to thank everyone who has encouraged me, assisted me, and prayed for me during the writing of this work, especially my spiritual parents, Dr. Jesse Duplantis and Dr. Cathy Duplantis. Special thanks to my wonderful wife Kathi for her love and dedication to the Lord and me. Thank you to a great staff for the wonderful job editing this book. Special thanks, as well, to all my friends who know the importance of a relationship with the person of the Holy Spirit and how He wants to operate in us and though us for the next move of God!

# CONTENTS

# INTRODUCTION

Through this 60-Day Devotional, I want to show you the role of the Holy Spirit in your life. He is the Spirit of Truth and wants to lead you into all truth! He is here to guide you and lead you into your destiny with God and assist you in fulfilling your Heavenly books.

God wants you to come into synchronization with Heaven as you learn to yield your tongue to the Holy Spirit and pray out God's perfect will for you and those around you. Learn to fully lean on and trust the person of the Holy Spirit. He was sent to help you, and He is never going to leave you. The Holy Spirit has made His home in you and now He wants to reveal God's heart to you; now is your time to receive from Him!

Enjoy the Devotional!

Dr. Kevin L. Zadai
Founder and President of Warrior Notes and Warrior Notes School of Ministry

*DR. KEVIN L. ZADAI*

# 60-DAY
# HOLY SPIRIT
# DEVOTIONAL

## DAY 1

## *The Holy Spirit in You*

*And I will pray the Father, and He will give
you another Helper, that He may abide with
you forever—the Spirit of truth, whom the
world cannot receive, because it neither sees
Him nor knows Him; but you know Him, for
He dwells with you and will be in you.*
—John 14:16-17

Did you know that you are never alone? The Holy Spirit goes with you wherever you go because He lives in you. Jesus said that the Holy Spirit would dwell with you. He is called your helper, and He is waiting for you to rely on Him. He's expecting your call.

God is synchronizing you with Heaven. He's willing to accomplish all that is on both your and the Father's heart. The Holy Spirit wants to help you fulfill the books that have been written about you in Heaven. He's guiding you today and causing you to triumph.

**Ask the Holy Spirit to show you the books that God has written about you. Pray about this and write what He reveals to you.**

_____

_____

_____

_____

_____

_____

_____

_____

_____

_____

_____

_____

_____

_____

# 60-DAY
# HOLY SPIRIT
# DEVOTIONAL

## DAY 2

## *Praying Out the Will of God*

*Likewise the Spirit also helps in our
weaknesses. For we do not know what we
should pray for as we ought, but the Spirit
Himself makes intercession for us with
groanings which cannot be uttered.*
—Romans 8:26

The Holy Spirit is able to pray you into God's
will. The way you do that is by yielding to the
Holy Spirit. We don't always know what to pray for,
but the Spirit knows. When we yield to Him and
pray in the Spirit, He prays the will of God through
us.   The Spirit intercedes on our behalf with
groanings. We don't know everything God has for
us, so we have to pray out the mysteries in the Spirit

and let The Holy Spirit interpret it to receive what God has for us.

In 1 Corinthians 2:11. Paul explains that no one discerns the thoughts of God except the Holy Spirit. God wants to transfer His thoughts to you, not in the understanding of your mind, but through the Spirit. He wants to pray the perfect will of God through you and then manifest His perfect will through your life. He wants you to fulfill your book and the plans He has for you!

**Yield to the Holy Spirit in prayer by praying in tongues. If you have not received tongues, ask Him to baptize you now. Stay in prayer as long as the Holy Spirit leads you. Write about your experience and what the Lord gives you as an interpretation and revelation.**

_____

_____

_____

_____

_____

_____

_____

_____

# 60-DAY
# HOLY SPIRIT
# DEVOTIONAL

## DAY 3

## *He is Trustworthy*

*Before you do anything, put your trust totally
in God and not in yourself. Then every plan
you make will succeed.*
—Proverbs 16:3 TPT

The Holy Spirit can help you in your weakness. The Spirit of God reveals the destiny and purpose of your life. He knows the truth, and that truth is setting you free. Yield to Him today because He wants to help you.

In the Old Testament, Solomon was very wise because he had the Holy Spirit's power. God gave him the gift of wisdom. Solomon reminds us that we need to trust in God and rely on the Holy Spirit, the Spirit of truth, within us. The Spirit of God is willing to assist you in your situation and show you the way to what God has for you. Nothing is impossible with Him. He has a pathway chosen for your deliverance, and there's already a solution.

In 1 Corinthians 10:13, Paul encourages us that when temptation comes our way, God always provides a way of escape so that we can bear up under it. You are going to encounter the guidance of the Holy Spirit today. The Holy Spirit is the Spirit of truth, which leads you into all truth. He wants to supply you with His power to overcome so you can walk in freedom.

**Seek the Holy Spirit's counsel and ask Him to give you wisdom for any concerns you have. Ask for solutions and His truth in the matter. Write down what He shows you.**

_____

_____

_____

_____

_____

_____

_____

_____

**DAY 4**

## *The Holy Spirit Knows Our Destiny*

*So we are convinced that every detail of our
lives is continually woven together for
good, for we are his lovers who have been
called to fulfill his designed purpose. For he
knew all about us before we were born, and
he destined us from the beginning to share
the likeness of his Son. This means the Son is
the oldest among a vast family of brothers
and sisters who will become just like him.*
—Romans 8:28-29 TPT

T he Holy Spirit has an essential role in your
life. His role is to show you your next steps
and lead you to your destiny. In John 14, Jesus
prepared for His leaving by promising that the
Father would send the Holy Spirit. Jesus explained

that the Holy Spirit would show us the things to come. The Holy Spirit's role is to show you where you are going.

In today's verse, Paul encourages us that every detail of our lives is interwoven with God's perfect will. He is bringing goodness into our lives, and He's been sent to help us. The Holy Spirit wants to show you personally that your destiny is in the palm of God's hand. He will never leave you; He is going to bring you to know the truth.

**With your destiny in His hands, ask God to reveal the next steps you can take to fulfill His purpose on the earth.**

_____

_____

_____

_____

_____

_____

_____

_____

_____

_____

# 60-DAY HOLY SPIRIT DEVOTIONAL

## DAY 5

## *The Holy Spirit Goes into Our Future*

*For I know the plans I have for you," says the LORD. "They are plans for good and not for disaster, to give you a future and a hope.*
—Jeremiah 29:11 NLT

God has plans for you that the Holy Spirit enforces. Even if we don't know everything that's up ahead of us, God does. If we synchronize ourselves with Heaven and submit to His plan and will for our lives, He will lead us into everything He has for us. It takes us trusting in Him.

In today's verse, we see Jeremiah relaying God's plan to Israel. He prophesied that God had a perfect and good plan with an expected good end. God had plans to prosper them. Israel ended up going

11

through terrible times, but God hadn't planned that for them. God wanted Israel to finish right. He planned that they would prosper. Even Jesus stood over Jerusalem a few nights before He was crucified and said, "How I long to gather you as a hen gathers her chicks under them." He said, "You didn't discern your day of visitation" (Luke 13:34,19:44). As believers, we have discerned our day of visitation.

Psalm 139 speaks about destiny and shares how God goes to our future and has already seen it. He caused us to be born into this world through our mother's womb. He is always there to fulfill your destiny.

**Cast your cares upon the Lord today. If anything is stopping you from believing that He wants to fulfill your destiny, release it to the Father. Then, submit to His plans and will for your life.**

_____

_____

_____

_____

_____

_____

_____

# 60-DAY
# HOLY SPIRIT
# DEVOTIONAL

## DAY 6

## *The Just Shall Live by Faith*

*You foolish Galatians! Who has bewitched you? Before your very eyes Jesus Christ was clearly portrayed as crucified. I would like to learn just one thing from you: Did you receive the Spirit by the works of the law, or by believing what you heard? Are you so foolish? After beginning by means of the Spirit, are you now trying to finish by means of the flesh?*
*—Galatians 3:1-3 NIV*

God has empowered you through His Word to remind you that you are justified by faith, *not* by your obedience to the law. The Holy Spirit is who empowers you. Do not allow yourself to get into the flesh to the point that you are striving. Don't allow the enemy or anyone else to trip you up and ruin your momentum with God. Instead, stay on the path of righteousness in the Spirit.

Through the born-again experience, God forgives and restores us to a rightful relationship with Him. Receive that you are forgiven and justified by faith. Pray in the Holy Spirit and build yourself up in the most Holy of faith (Jude 1:20). Remain obedient to what the Spirit of God and His Word are saying. When evil spirits come, their purpose is to get you to strive in the flesh and slow down your momentum. Don't fall for it! Instead, be vigilant and aware of these tactics. God is the opposite; He wants to empower you to finish your race. Use discernment and stay in the Holy Spirit. You will overcome!

**Seek the Holy Spirit concerning anything you may be trying to obtain through your own efforts in the flesh. Turn it over to Him and trust in the Lord.**

_____

_____

_____

_____

_____

# 60-DAY
# HOLY SPIRIT
# DEVOTIONAL

## DAY 7

## *The Holy Spirit Gives Us Hope*

*And this hope is not a disappointing fantasy,
because we can now experience the endless
love of God cascading into our hearts
through the Holy Spirit who lives in us!*
*—Romans 5:5 TPT*

God has given us hope in our Spirit. He has given us dreams and desires that He wants to fulfill in our lives. He hasn't given us a disappointing fantasy. God wants us to achieve a specific plan and purpose for our lives, but it has to be done in the Spirit.

The Lord wants to work within you to pursue the dreams you have. Rely on Him to help you overcome anything holding you back from

15

believing. He wants to help you take the necessary steps to get you where He wants you to be. In the meantime, don't allow anything to disappoint or discourage you from pursuing your dreams. God put these dreams there, and He wants to accomplish them in your life because He loves and cares for you. He has placed a hope in you that won't disappoint. It's an eternal hope that causes you to continue day by day. Be encouraged; the Holy Spirit is with you to see this through!

**Today in prayer, seek the Holy Spirit's guidance in stepping into what He wants you to accomplish here on earth. Ask Him to show you what it looks like to live and operate in these things. Write down what He shows or tells you about taking the next step toward your goals.**

_____

_____

_____

_____

_____

_____

_____

_____

# 60-DAY
# HOLY SPIRIT
# DEVOTIONAL

## DAY 8

## *You Have Full Authority*

*But you belong to God, my dear children.
You have already won a victory over those
people, because the Spirit who lives in you is
greater than the spirit who lives in the
world.*
*—John 4:4 NLT*

Did you know that the Holy Spirit gives you the boldness and authority to cast out devils, and that they actually want to leave when they encounter you? When you're full of the Spirit, the devils want nothing to do with you. The Spirit in you is greater than the spirit of this world. It enables you to move in signs and wonders. Mark 16:17 says, "And these signs will follow those who believe: In My name, they will cast out demons; they will speak with new tongues."

Be encouraged that when you show up there are battle lines being drawn. You're already in a war because you're here in this world, but the Spirit of God is in you, and He wants to drive out devils, and they know it (Mark 3:15). The Holy Spirit has a command about Him, and He's in you, so wherever you go, His power is flowing through you. God's authority goes with you wherever He sends you in your realm of influence. The power that rose Jesus from the dead is dwelling in you. May you see the hope to which you've been called and walk in authority against the evil spirits of this world.

**Today when you go out in the world, be aware that the authority and power you carry gives you victory over demons and the ability to walk in miracles, signs, and wonders. Put it to use today and write down how you triumphed over darkness.**

_____

_____

_____

_____

_____

# 60-DAY HOLY SPIRIT DEVOTIONAL

## DAY 9

### *The Holy Spirit is a Person*

*"But I will send you the Advocate—the Spirit of truth. He will come to you from the Father and will testify all about me."*
*—John 15:26 NLT*

Jesus said He would send one like Himself and that He would be a friend, cause us to remember everything that Jesus said, and show us things to come (John 14:26). Jesus sent the Holy Spirit back, and He is an actual person.

The Holy Spirit is beautiful. He is an advocate, an attorney, a lawyer, a counselor, and standby. He's the one that strengthens and encourages you. He not only argues your case, but He also gives you wisdom, understanding, and counsel about what the

Father is saying and doing. Every day with Him is an adventure and a journey.

It doesn't have to be where you're always in warfare trying to figure out what's going on. You can rest and trust in Him. The Holy Spirit is just like Jesus. He's giving you the wisdom and instruction today because He wants to change History through you. Just yield to Him and let Him guide you.

**In what way(s) do you need the Holy Spirit to help you? Do you need an advocate, counselor, lawyer, or friend? Go into prayer and invite Him to come and share with you how He can assist you. Write about the ways He came through for you in prayer or your day today.**

_____

_____

_____

_____

_____

_____

_____

_____

_____

_____

# 60-DAY
# HOLY SPIRIT
# DEVOTIONAL

## DAY 10

### *You Know Him Intimately*

*And I will ask the Father and he will give
you another Savior, the Holy Spirit of Truth,
who will be to you a friend just like me—and
he will never leave you. The world won't
receive him because they can't see him or
know him. But you know him intimately
because he remains with you and will live
inside you.*
*—John 14:16-17 TPT*

The Spirit of Truth is your friend. He wants to
help you and encourage you. He wants to
reveal this to you so that you know Him intimately.
He is just like Jesus, and He's never going to leave
you. That means no matter what happens the Holy
Spirit is going to be there for you.

The reality is, He wants to counsel you and guide you. The Holy Spirit will show you the things to come. He reveals the things of God because He knows God's heart. The Holy Spirit has made His home in you, and He's abiding in you. He's not worried about your day at all. He's going to take care of your problems. When you get to Heaven, you're going to find out how many things He prevented from happening because the Holy Spirit was at work. He was helping all along to guide and lead you. Trust in Him to show you what He knows so that you can go about your day with confidence.

**In prayer, meditate on today's verse. As you go about your day, ask the Holy Spirit to show you how true this verse is. Write out the verse and meditate on it throughout your day, then write down what you experienced.**

_____

_____

_____

_____

_____

_____

_____

**DAY 11**

## _Diligently Seek Him_

_Demons also came out of many of them.
Knowing that Jesus was the Anointed One,
the demons shouted while coming out, "You
are the Messiah, the Son of El Shaddai!" But
Jesus rebuked them and commanded them to
be silent.
—Luke 4:41 TPT_

The Holy Spirit is purposed on advancing the Kingdom of God. Through Jesus, He accomplished this by driving out devils, and He wants to do it through you. Jesus was anointed, and the demons knew who He was. As they were cast out in the above verse, the demons shouted and said, "You are the Messiah, the son of El Shaddai."

But then we see that Jesus rebuked them and commanded them to be silent.

He wants you to get to a place where demons know who you are, and they vacate. Hebrews 11:6 says that God is a rewarder of those who diligently seek Him. By building yourself up in the most Holy of Faith, praying in the Spirit, and remaining in the love of God, you will be transformed by the renewing of your mind (Jude 1:20, Romans 12:2). Meditate on His Word day and night because there's a power that's being developed in you. It's a power from Heaven that happens when God overcomes you.

There's a point when He's overcome you so much that the evil spirits know it. They know that they have to go, so they start to manifest around you. Don't be discouraged when people act up. If evil spirits are near a person or in their emotions, then they will want to manifest. It's part of your life that you walk in the Spirit and drive out devils, so stay built up and walk in boldness.

Ask the Holy Spirit to show you the power you walk in. Go out and share God's love with someone today.

_____

_____

_____

_____

_____

_____

_____

_____

_____

_____

_____

_____

_____

_____

_____

_____

_____

_____

_____

**DAY 12**

## *<u>The Resurrection Power in You</u>*

*"And these signs shall follow them that*
*believe; In my name shall they cast out*
*devils; they shall speak with new tongues;"*
*—Mark 16:17 KJV*

The Spirit of God rose Jesus from the dead, and that Resurrection power is living in you because you have the Holy Spirit. He is the Resurrection life of God, and He wants to raise the dead. The Holy Spirit is willing to resurrect what's dead in any situation.

It might not be a literal person that needs to be resurrected; it may be a dead situation in your life that is in need of this power. There may be

27

relationships or financial problems happening that the Holy Spirit wants to bring to life. Allow Him to use you to speak from your spirit into your bank accounts, your health, finances, and relationships.

Speak life into these areas where you need Resurrection power. He wants you to raise dead things in the marketplace, at your job, and in your future. We need to speak into these places and see dead things raised to life again. The Resurrection power of Jesus Christ is the Spirit of God who lives in you, so be encouraged.


**ACTIVATION: In prayer, connect to the Holy Spirit, and speak life into every area that needs Resurrection power. Call those dead things back to life. Record what you encounter.**

_____

_____

_____

_____

_____

_____

_____

_____

_____

# 60-DAY
# HOLY SPIRIT
# DEVOTIONAL

**DAY 13**

## *Baptized in Fire*

*Those who repent I baptize with water, but
there is coming a man after me who is more
powerful than I. In fact, I'm not even worthy
enough to pick up his sandals. He will
submerge you into union with the Spirit of
Holiness and with a raging fire!*
—*Matthew 3:11 TPT*

God wants to baptize us, immerse us, and
merge us with Him in fire. When He baptizes
in fire, He purifies and sanctifies us. We are in
union with the Spirit of Holiness. The Spirit of
Holiness is fire, and it's burning in you. There's fire
throughout Heaven. The angels are on fire, the Altar

is on fire, and the seraphim are on fire. There is fire on the Sapphire floor.

In Heaven, all things are separate and Holy in God's sight. God has separated us and baptized us with the Holy Spirit and fire. We can rejoice in our sanctification and union with Him.

**Meditate on the fact that you are baptized into union with the Holy Spirit and with fire. Let Him show you what that means and how powerful it is. Write down what you encounter in the secret place with Him.**

_____

_____

_____

_____

_____

_____

_____

_____

_____

_____

_____

# 60-DAY
# HOLY SPIRIT
# DEVOTIONAL

**DAY 14**

## *He Reveals Himself to Us*

*But it was to us that God revealed these things by his Spirit. For his Spirit searches out everything and shows us God's deep secrets.*
*—1 Corinthians 2:10 NLT*

T he Spirit of God reveals the Lord. Jesus is the Lord, and He said that the One who was coming would remind us of things that He said and that He would show us the future.

The Holy Spirit knows the secrets of God, and He wants to share them with you. Yield to Him because there are many things He wants to show you. Every day is like a treasure hunt with the Lord, and He wants to reveal these hidden nuggets to you.

Give Him permission to go on a journey with you. He wants to bring forth the mysteries of the kingdom and the Father. God gave us the Holy Spirit as the Spirit of Revelation to help us understand and have wisdom. My prayer for you today is that your ears and eyes are opened so that you may receive all that He has for you.

**Take time and yield to the Holy Spirit in prayer. Open yourself up to receiving His revelation. Ask Him to reveal the mysteries of Heaven. As you go out today, pay attention to what He shows you. Continue to yield to Him throughout the day. Write about your experience.**

_____

_____

_____

_____

_____

_____

_____

_____

_____

_____

**DAY 15**

## *Spirit of Reality*

*Who his own self bare our sins in his own
body on the tree, that we, being dead to sins,
should live unto righteousness: by whose
stripes ye were healed.*
—1 Peter 2:24 KJV

There is a higher law that supersedes facts. Peter reveals that when he quoted Isaiah 53. The prophet Isaiah said the Messiah would take stripes upon His back, and through those stripes, we were healed. Peter quotes this and says, "Now by His stripes, ye *were* healed." His quote represents a higher law, and that law supersedes the facts.

For example, you may be encountering sickness or pain, but God says, "The absolute truth is that I paid for your healing!" It's a fact that you may be experiencing pain, and no one denies that, but the higher law is saying that Jesus took stripes on His back for that pain, and it supersedes what you're experiencing. The reality is you were healed on that day Jesus took those stripes.

In Heaven, we have absolute truth. Absolute truth is not disputable or compromised in any way. We may have the facts down here, but they're disputable because God is greater, and He has greater authority. God has established truth, so we can know it, and it will set us free.

**Pray intimately with the Holy Spirit about how the truth has set you free. Release and submit any thought that opposes that He is the healer. Thank Him for giving you His Spirit of Truth; receive His healing. Write about His love for you.**

_____

_____

_____

_____

_____

_____

_____

_____

# 60-DAY
# HOLY SPIRIT
# DEVOTIONAL

**DAY 16**

## *Spirit of Reality Part 2*

*"And I will send you the Divine Encourager from the very presence of my Father. He will come to you, the Spirit of Truth, emanating from the Father, and he will speak to you about me. And you will tell everyone the truth about me, for you have walked with me from the start."*
—John 15:26-27 TPT

The word truth also means *reality*. The Spirit of truth *is* the Spirit of reality. You may think you truly know something, but God wants to show you the absolute truth about it because He is the Spirit of reality. He only knows the truth. You may have been thinking you knew the truth the whole time, but then you find out that what you knew was merely a fact.

Science is based on facts, but scientists often discover something else that supersedes the previous assumptions and then they revise their "facts." You may feel pain, and that is a fact, but the truth is you were healed! The absolute truth is that God paid for your healing. The Spirit of Truth supersedes and goes above the facts. Today God is speaking His reality into every area of your life. He is prospering you and causing you to be healed and delivered. His reality and truth are alive within you, so trust and believe in Him.

**Acknowledge that Jesus has already healed you and come into agreement with the Spirit of Reality. Use the Word of God to respond to any "facts" that do not align with God and His kingdom.**

_____

_____

_____

_____

_____

_____

## DAY 17

### *He Leads Us in Prayer*

*They were all filled and equipped with the
Holy Spirit and were inspired to speak in
tongues—empowered by the Spirit to speak
in languages they had never learned!*
*—Acts 2:4 TPT*

When we yield to the Holy Spirit, we are
yielding to the One who will lead us into
prayer. If He's the One that's leading us into prayer,
we're going to receive our answers because the
Holy Spirit leads us into all truth. When the people
in the upper room yielded to the spirit in the Book
of Acts, they were able to do something beyond
what they could do before. The Holy Spirit leads us
and helps us to pray out the perfect will of God.
When we yield to Him, He delivers us from

ourselves. He causes us to do something we couldn't do before, and He leads us into the divine life, which causes us to be delivered of our cravings and sinful nature.

> *And the Holy Spirit helps us in our weakness. For example, we don't know what God wants us to pray for. But the Holy Spirit prays for us with groanings that cannot be expressed in words.*
>
> *—Romans 8:26*

> *Let me emphasize this: As you yield to the dynamic life and power of the Holy Spirit, you will abandon the cravings of your self-life.*
>
> *—Galatians 5:16*

**Yield to the Holy Spirit in prayer. Give Him full permission to have His way. Sit, and wait until He reveals what to pray for. Tongues or groanings will rise up within you. Let it out.**

_____

_____

_____

_____

_____

# 60-DAY
# HOLY SPIRIT
# DEVOTIONAL

## DAY 18

## *The Holy Spirit Debriefs Us*

*So above all, constantly seek God's
kingdom and his righteousness, then all
these less important things will be given to
you abundantly.*
*—Matthew 6:33 TPT*

The Spirit of God wants to give us information about what's happening in the Kingdom. He wants to tell us things in the morning when we wake up and at the end of the day. He wants to debrief us, and go over some things. I'm always asking the Lord what I could have done better. At the beginning of the day, I say, "Lord, whatever it is that you need to get across to me, please let me know because I'm not going to be able to understand or know everything."

I turn myself in and God seems to always work it out. When things don't go right, there's always another day. He will always help us out. God wants us to seek the face of Jesus, to seek His kingdom, and seek His righteousness. Then all these lesser things that we need, God is going to make sure that we have those things in abundant supply. They're going to come to us because we don't look to them; we look to our Heavenly Father, who is well pleased and wants to give us everything we need.

> *For the kingdom of God is not a matter of rules about food and drink, but is in the realm of the Holy Spirit, filled with righteousness, peace, and joy.*
> —*Romans 14:17 TPT*

**Today, seek the Holy Spirit in prayer. Talk to Him about the intimate details of your life. Ask Him what He thinks about what you're doing and ways you can grow. He will guide you. Write about it.**

_____

_____

_____

_____

_____

**DAY 19**

## *The Power to Enrich You*

*"How enriched you are when persecuted for
doing what is right! For then you experience
the realm of Heaven's kingdom."*
—Matthew 5:10 TPT

We often think that we've done something wrong when we get persecuted and people say wrong things about us, but we have to realize that we are to be happy and joyful when we are persecuted. Be joyful when you are excluded from things because great is your reward in Heaven!

We forget that Jesus said that you should be overwhelmed with joy when you're persecuted because you've been counted worthy. As you go out today, if you're excluded, and you don't feel like you fit in, remember they rejected Jesus, and they're going to reject you. The reward is great because you're being persecuted for the kingdom of God. Everything about your life down here is with God, and He wants to provide for you. The Holy Spirit is right there to reinforce this, so be of good cheer because Jesus has overcome the world (John 16:33).

**Pray about your day and ask God how He wants to use you in the marketplace. When you go out, stand for righteousness if given the opportunity be bold in your faith. Ask Him to show you a glimpse of what you're going to encounter. Make it a great day!**

_____

_____

_____

_____

_____

_____

_____

_____

_____

_____

**DAY 20**

## *<u>The Key to Your Revelation</u>*

*But the Helper, the Holy Spirit, whom the
Father will send in my name, he will teach
you all things and bring to your
remembrance all that I have said to you.
—John 14:26 ESV*

The Holy Spirit is your key. He is the revealer,
and He has all the keys to the kingdom. In
other words, He is the key to your revelation. The
Holy Spirit is the only One that we have right now.
Jesus is seated at the right hand of God, and the
Father is seated there on His throne. The angels are
there, and they're sent here to help us, but the Holy
Spirit is not only on the earth, but He is also within
you as a believer.  He wants to talk to us about

Jesus and bring into remembrance the things that Jesus said.

> *"But when the Helper comes, whom I shall send to you from the Father, the Spirit of truth who proceeds from the Father, He will testify of Me."*
> —John 15:26 NKJV

We have the One who can reveal Jesus to us. He wants to reveal the future, and remind us of everything that Jesus said. He's going to speak and lead us into all truth. The Spirit of Truth is the One that we have right now, and you cannot fail if you would just yield to Him.

**Yield and talk to the Holy Spirit in prayer about the ways He wants to reveal Himself to you. Ask Him to show you today. Throughout your day just yield to Him and press in.**

_____

_____

_____

_____

_____

_____

_____

# 60-DAY
# HOLY SPIRIT
# DEVOTIONAL

## DAY 21

### *Holy Spirit the Lawyer*

*Now the Lord is the Spirit, and where the*
*Spirit of the Lord is, there is freedom.*
*— 2 Corinthians 3:17 NIV*

The Holy Spirit is an advocate, which is another word for lawyer. He is an attorney that gets what He wants and gets the case won. He is a lawyer that has never lost a case. As long as we are submissive to Him, He's going to win for us. Whatever is going on in your life, submit it to the Holy Spirit; give it to God. The Spirit of God wants to take care of anything that has to do with you.

We know we have the Holy Spirit inside of us, so we have freedom. We have liberty right inside of us. You can begin to feel yourself getting set free right now because the Holy Spirit doesn't know bondage. He only knows liberty.

The Spirit of the Lord is the advocate, the lawyer that wants to win your case. Trust in Him to argue your case, take over, and win for you. When He intervenes, speaks on our behalf and takes us before the throne, we will receive everything we ask for.

**Submit to the Holy Spirit in prayer and give Him every area or concern that you are seeking justice. Press in and listen to how He guides you and gives you wisdom in your situation. He will instruct you on what to do and say to see freedom in your situation.**

_____

_____

_____

_____

_____

_____

_____

_____

_____

# 60-DAY
# HOLY SPIRIT
# DEVOTIONAL

## DAY 22

### *He Stays with You Forever*

*Nevertheless I tell you the truth. It is to your advantage that I go away; for if I do not go away, the Helper will not come to you; but if I depart, I will send Him to you. And when He has come, He will convict the world of sin, and of righteousness, and of judgment: of sin, because they do not believe in Me; of righteousness, because I go to My Father and you see Me no more; of judgment, because the ruler of this world is judged. "I still have many things to say to you, but you cannot bear them now. However, when He, the Spirit of truth, has come, He will guide you into all truth; for He will not speak on His own authority, but whatever He hears He will speak; and He will tell you things to come. He will glorify Me, for He will take of what is Mine and declare it to you. All things that the Father has are Mine. Therefore I said that He will take of Mine and declare it to you.*
—John 16:7-15 NKJV

The role of the Holy Spirit in your life is that He has been told to stay with you forever. Jesus said, "I'm leaving, but I'm going to send one who's going to be with you forever." No matter what you feel today, the Holy Spirit has not left you. He is right there with you, and if you yield to Him inside of you, rivers of living water are going to flow out from you. God has an intimate relationship that He's already established for you with the Holy Spirit. He's going to help you in every single way.

**Press into the Holy Spirit within you. Let Him reveal the rivers of living water inside of you. What is He showing you about His love for you?**

_____

_____

_____

_____

_____

_____

_____

_____

_____

_____

_____

_____

# 60-DAY
# HOLY SPIRIT
# DEVOTIONAL

## DAY 23

## *He Stands in Your Future*

*You've gone into my future to prepare the
way, and in kindness you follow behind me
to spare me from the harm of my past. You
have laid your hand on me!*
—Psalm 139:5 TPT

God wants you to yield to the Holy Spirit to
where you are firmly convinced about your
destiny. Jesus is standing in your future right now.
Yield to Him so that He can lead and guide you in
your destiny.

The Lord is standing in your future. He has paved a
way to your future and He's standing there. He's
making sure that you are going to arrive at your

destiny. He's making sure that all the plans He has for you succeed because that's what He wants for you.

God doesn't lose, and He doesn't want you to lose either. The angels of the Lord have been sent to escort you. The word of the Lord over you is that you are going to make it, and you're going to be fine. Everything is going to work out for you!

**Yield to the Holy Spirit in prayer. Let Him show you a glimpse of your future. Commit to the path of righteousness where the Lord orders every step you take. Do as He says because each step leads you there. Write out what He reveals to you.**

_____

_____

_____

_____

_____

_____

_____

_____

_____

_____

**DAY 24**

## *A Higher Vantage Point*

*Therefore if the Son makes you free, you
shall be free indeed.
—John 8:36 NKJV*

The Holy Spirit wants to shift our perspective and give us a new way of looking at things from a higher vantage point. The Spirit of Truth is going to lead you into all truth. When the Holy Spirit comes, He changes everything. Wherever the Holy Spirit is, there is freedom. Jesus said, "He who the Son sets free is free indeed."

It makes me think about the woman at the well. She was just sitting there doing her thing, and began talking to Jesus. She had no idea who He was, but by the end of that conversation, she thought differently, didn't she? Everything about her was lifted and she could see something that she didn't see before. She didn't discern who she was talking to at first. Jesus was the source, her creator. She encountered her creator that day, and it changed her life forever.

He wants to talk to you and set you free. He wants to give you a different perspective. Be encouraged because the Lord will give you a high vantage point so that you can see things as He sees them.

**Pray and meditate on how the Holy Spirit will lift you into a higher place so that you can see the ways of the Lord and enter into what God has for you. Let Him show you. Write about it below.**

_____

_____

_____

_____

_____

_____

_____

_____

_____

_____

# 60-DAY

# HOLY SPIRIT
# DEVOTIONAL

**DAY 25**

## *The Creator Lives in You*

*For those who are led by the Spirit of God*
*are the children of God.*
*—Romans 8:14 NIV*

The creator of the universe lives inside of you. The Holy Spirit, who rose Jesus from the dead —the power of God, lives in you. All the testimonies of the prophets and the apostles, Moses, and all the men and women of God who have come before us; their testimony was that God was with them in a mighty way. Jesus said that there was no one as great as John the Baptist, but everyone would be greater than John from then on (Matthew 11:11). That's us. The prophets had the privilege of speaking things into existence. They foretold what was going to happen in the future. Jesus fulfilled all those Old Testament prophecies in the New Testament. He was the fulfillment of everything that was laid before Him.

Those who are led by the Spirit of God are Sons of God. He is leading us, and we're at the end of the age. We're the ones they were prophesying about at the end. We're looking back at the cross and proclaiming that God is faithful. The Holy Spirit is going to lead you into all truth so that you are the fulfillment of prophecy. Those who have gone before us were looking forward to this day when you would be here to fulfill your destiny. Know that you are a part of history, and you're going to change history!

*But you have received the Holy Spirit, and he lives within you, so you don't need anyone to teach you what is true. For the Spirit teaches you everything you need to know, and what he teaches is true—it is not a lie. So just as he has taught you, remain in fellowship with Christ.*

*—1 John 2:27 NLT*

**Begin to prophesy into your own life from what God shows you. Be bold today in the marketplace and prophecy what He directs you to say to others.**

_____

_____

_____

_____

_____

_____

_____

_____

_____

_____

_____

_____

_____

_____

_____

_____

_____

_____

_____

**DAY 26**

## *Choose Your Words Wisely*

*But I say to you that for every idle word men may speak, they will give account of it in the day of judgment.*
*—Matthew 12:36 NKJV*

Jesus was proclaiming to the disciples and Pharisees that they would be held accountable for every idle word that comes out of their mouths. That was not only for them but for us today. It is so important that we watch our words and choose them wisely. The Holy Spirit wants to borrow your tongue to speak because He wants to use you in a mighty way.

*Death and life are in the power of the tongue, And those who love it will eat its fruit.*

—Proverbs 18:21

Your words produce fruit, and you can eat from it. When you say something, if you believe it in your heart and you say it with your mouth, you're going to have it. That's why you can speak to mountains and mountains move (Mark 11:23). Jesus said it's the same way when you pray. You should already believe that you received it before you pray, and you're going to have it (Matthew 21:22).

*"Let the words of my mouth, and the meditation of my heart, be acceptable in thy sight, O LORD, my strength, and my redeemer."*

—Psalms 19:14 KJV

*There is one who speaks like the piercings of a sword, But the tongue of the wise promotes health.*

—Proverbs 12:18

Submit your tongue and repent for any idle words spoken. Begin fresh today; allow Him to speak through you, declaring the truth over your life, your health, and your future. Remember, you will eat from the fruit of your words. Speak good things over others and share it.

_____

_____

_____

_____

_____

_____

_____

_____

_____

_____

_____

_____

_____

_____

_____

_____

*DR. KEVIN L. ZADAI*

# 60-DAY
# HOLY SPIRIT
# DEVOTIONAL

**DAY 27**

## *Be Imitators of God*

*But the Holy Spirit produces this kind of fruit in our lives: love, joy, peace, patience, kindness, goodness, faithfulness, gentleness, and self-control. There is no law against these things!*
*—Galatians 5:22-23 NLT*

The Spirit of God produces many gifts that are evident in a believer who yields to the Spirit. The gifts of the Spirit are the workings of Jesus Christ coming through us (1 Corinthians 12,14). While they are important here on earth, I saw in Heaven that we give them back. They are not ours to keep because they are gifts.

God is most concerned about our character. The character God gives us is through the things that we endure. It comes when we choose to live rightly. The fruit of the Spirit is really the character and personality of God, but it also becomes your personality and character (Galatians 5:22-33).

That's why we yield to the Spirit and allow God to use us in the gifts of the Spirit. As we do this, we'll begin to experience God's personality. That's what He wants for us, for His personality to overcome us to the point where we become imitators of God. We want to be imitators of God as dearly loved children of God (Ephesians 5:1). Today, let love, joy, peace, patience, kindness, goodness, faithfulness, gentleness, and self-control rule in your life.

**If there's any sin you're dealing with, repent and turn from it fully. When you are submitted to the Holy Spirit, you will see His fruit produced in you. Yield to the Spirit of God. Allow Him to show you His perfect ways. Write about what you encountered.**

_____

_____

_____

_____

## DAY 28

## *<u>The Holy Spirit Wants to<br>Shift Your Atmosphere</u>*

*After they prayed, the place where they were
meeting was shaken. And they were all filled
with the Holy Spirit and spoke the word of
God boldly.*
*—Acts 4:31 NIV*

The Holy Spirit will bring an atmosphere into
your life in a particular way that will shift
your perspective. He wants you to have a new view
of what God is saying. It may come through as an
angel visitation or the breath of the Holy Spirit. It
might be the Word of God becoming real to you or
someone else coming to minister to you. Whichever
way the Holy Spirit chooses to bring that

atmosphere to your life, expect a change in your attitude that will cause you to flourish and grow.

Many things that happen around you are because of warfare. It's not necessarily because you're doing something wrong or right; it is due to this broken world. You can't judge how well you're doing by what's happening around you. The kingdom of God is in Heaven, but it's also within you. The Holy Spirit wants to change your atmosphere so that you can grow and see what God sees. He wants to show you what He sees in you and your future. He wants to show you what He has always thought of you because He's heavily invested in you. God sent His Son to die for you. You are highly valued and esteemed in Heaven, and God brags about you. Be encouraged; the saints are cheering you on!

**Yield to The Holy Spirit throughout your day. Watch what He does today as He opens up the atmosphere for you to receive a new and life-giving reality. Write about your day.**

_____

_____

_____

_____

_____

# 60-DAY
# HOLY SPIRIT
# DEVOTIONAL

**DAY 29**

## *Let the Spirit Dictate what You Believe*

*But the Helper, the Holy Spirit, whom the
Father will send in My name, He will teach you
all things, and bring to your remembrance all
things that I said to you.*
—John 14:16

W hen we yield to the Holy Spirit, it gives us a new view on life. He is able to help us through discouragement when we've received bad news or negative reports. We need Him to correct us and tell us what our perception is supposed to be. I always check in with the Holy Spirit when I hear bad news, or when I see something going on that's not right. If I encounter pain in my body or something's wrong, I always check in with God. I don't allow myself to get depressed or to be discouraged. I always let the Holy Spirit dictate what I believe. The Word of God is our stronghold. We have to stare at His Word and not at our circumstances. The Holy Spirit came as a helper to help and counsel us, and He's going to tell us what the truth is, so don't let these circumstances dictate the truth.

The Holy Spirit is the One who's going to teach you all things, not the circumstances, not the evil spirits, not family members. God has sent the Holy Spirit as your teacher, and He's the One that's going to help you. Jesus said, "I'm going to send you the advocate" (John 15:26). He's the Spirit of Truth and the One who will say what the truth is. The advocate will tell you whether your circumstance is God or not. He will tell you the direction you should go. Trust in Him —He is elevating your perception so that you know the truth, and it sets you free!

**Yield to the Holy Spirit as a way of living. Seek Him for your answers and respond with His replies. From this day forward, do everything from Him**

_____

_____

_____

_____

# 60-DAY
# HOLY SPIRIT
# DEVOTIONAL

## DAY 30

## _Spoken Faith Activates the Holy Spirit_

_But we continue to preach because we have
the same kind of faith the psalmist had when
he said, "I believed in God, so I spoke."_
—2 Corinthians 4:13 NLT

There is a place where we need to be responsible and accountable to speak what God is speaking. Doing this will activate the Holy Spirit. There are times where you need to speak and voice from your spirit because you are the authority on this earth. There are times where nothing is happening, and it's because you need to pray.

Did you know that you are an ambassador that has been sent by God? All believers are sent ones because we have the Holy Spirit within us. We are the body of Christ on the earth. If you believe that what you say shall come to pass, it shall come to pass—it's called "speaking to mountains." You have to believe in your heart that what you say with your mouth is going to come to pass, and then it will.

> *So Jesus answered and said to them, "Have faith in God. For assuredly, I say to you, whoever says to this mountain, 'Be removed and be cast into the sea,' and does not doubt in his heart, but believes that those things he says will be done, he will have whatever he says.*
>
> *—Mark 11:22-23*

**Activation:** From your spirit, speak out the destiny of God over your life. Speak out of faith, and watch how He manifests in power through you. Write out some declarations you made today.

_____

_____

_____

_____

_____

_____

## DAY 31

## *He Sets You up for a Miracle*

*Then God added his witness to theirs. He
validated their ministry with signs,
astonishing wonders, all kinds of powerful
miracles, and by the gifts of the Holy Spirit,
which he distributed as he desired.*
—Hebrew 2:4 TPT

The Holy Spirit wants you to allow Him to set
you up for a miracle. You can pray in the
Spirit and believe in your heart, and God can set
you up for something special today. Did you know
that He always wants you to minister to people?
God can answer your prayers for others very
quickly. If you ask, then you're going to receive.
You can always see answered prayers by asking
God to use you and asking for His wisdom.

God validated the ministry of the apostles with signs and wonders following. You have a ministry, and God wants to speak through you. He wants you to engage with Him because He wants to set you up for a miracle. Believe that God will use you to speak to others and minister to them. When you speak His Word, He will confirm it with signs and wonders following. According to 1 Corinthians 12:11, the Spirit has placed gifts in you severally; God decided which giftings you would have. You have several gifts inside you that God wants to be activated. My prayer for you is that they are activated, and God sets you up for a miracle today and that it's validated with signs, miracles, and wonders following, in Jesus' name!

**Pray about how the Holy Spirit wants to use you in different ways to reach souls. When you go out, apply what He has shown you, and see how the Lord validates your ministry through miracles, signs, and wonders.**

_____

_____

_____

_____

_____

# 60-DAY
# HOLY SPIRIT
# DEVOTIONAL

## DAY 32

## *Walk in the Spirit*

*I say then: Walk in the Spirit, and you shall*
*not fulfill the lust of the flesh.*
*—Galatians 5:16*

Jesus taught us how to walk in the Spirit. He showed us that what He did through His ministry was only from the Father. Everything He said was from the Father. Paul said that those who are the Sons of God are the ones who walk in the Spirit. Those who are led and walk in the Spirit are the Sons of God (Romans 8:14). That is who we are. We have the Spirit inside of us, and we can yield to Him, and He will give us the ability to walk in the Spirit, do His will, and be led by Him.

71

*For those who live according to the flesh set their minds on the things of the flesh, but those who live according to the Spirit, the things of the Spirit.*

—*Romans 8:5*

We have the manifestation of walking in the Spirit to do His will that allows the Spirit to take us into our destiny. We will prosper and triumph in Him.

**Yield to Spirit in prayer. As you go out, be determined that everything you do and say comes from the Father. Make this a lifestyle of yielding to Him and living from Him.**

_____

_____

_____

_____

_____

_____

_____

_____

_____

_____

_____

**DAY 33**

## *Into the Supernatural*

*Those who are motivated by the flesh only
pursue what benefits themselves. But those
who live by the impulses of the Holy Spirit
are motivated to pursue spiritual realities.*
—*Romans 8:5 TPT*

Yielding to the Holy Spirit ushers us into the realm of the supernatural. The Holy Spirit is already in that realm, and He wants to provide a pathway for you to enter. He will coach you, showing you the way into truth by lighting up the path. Whatever you think you can't do, the Holy Spirit will show you that He can. Just believe that the Lord is going to usher you into the supernatural.

He takes what is impossible and makes it possible for you. By the Holy Spirit, He empowers you to do the impossible. Have the type of faith in you that fails not (Luke 22:32). Be inclined by the Holy Spirit's ability and not your own and yield to Him.

**Pray in the Spirit and remain yielded to Him no matter what goes on around you. Talk to the Holy Spirit throughout your day and write about your encounters in the supernatural realm.**

_____

_____

_____

_____

_____

_____

_____

_____

_____

_____

_____

_____

_____

_____

_____

# 60-DAY
# HOLY SPIRIT
# DEVOTIONAL

## DAY 34

## *The Holy Spirit Unveils Secrets*

*But when the truth-giving Spirit comes, he
will unveil the reality of every truth within
you. He won't speak on his own, but only
what he hears from the Father, and he will
reveal prophetically to you what is to come.
He will glorify me on the earth, for he will
receive from me what is mine and reveal it
to you. Everything that belongs to the Father
belongs to me—that's why I say that the
Divine Encourager will receive what is mine
and reveal it to you.*
*—John 16:13-15 TPT*

We know that the truth sets us free. The Holy Spirit is the one who unveils the truth, and He's unveiling the secrets of God's kingdom to you. You might not know what the truth is today, but He wants to reveal it to you, and it will set you free.

The Holy Spirit is inside of you, and you can communicate with Him as often as you like. He is speaking what the Father is saying, and He wants to share His secrets with you so that you know what to do. The Father has great plans for you. Be encouraged and look to Him within!

**Connect with the Holy Spirit in prayer and listen to what the Spirit unveils to you. Write down what you hear or see in the Spirit.**

_____

_____

_____

_____

_____

_____

_____

_____

_____

_____

# 60-DAY
# HOLY SPIRIT
# DEVOTIONAL

## DAY 35

## *If it's not From the Spirit, it Will not Work*

*It is the Spirit who gives life; the flesh
profits nothing. The words that I speak to
you are spirit, and they are life.*
—*John 6:63 NKJV*

In the Spirit, you can win! However, you cannot produce something from the Spirit in the flesh; you must submit the flesh. If it wasn't from the Spirit, it's not going to work, and it won't last. Remember that everything you do has to originate from truth.

When Jesus went around speaking to the crowds, people said, "No man ever spoke like this man!" (John 7:46). He wasn't like the Pharisees; He spoke words of life. When Jesus spoke, it was only what

His Father was telling Him to say (John 12:49). He spoke from His heart and spirit, and this is what produces life. You cannot produce life in the flesh—the works of man in the flesh profits nothing (John 6:63).

Under the law, people tried to behave. They had different laws they had to obey, and it was just futile because no one could fully keep the law. Then Jesus came, and He fulfilled everything. All the requirements of the law were met through Jesus. He's asking us to produce life by living in the Spirit and allowing the Spirit of the Lord to set us free.

**In prayer, submit to the Holy Spirit. If you've been trying to make things happen in your own strength, now is the time to give it up and get under the influence of the Spirit. Yield to His Spirit and let Him show you.**

_____

_____

_____

_____

_____

_____

_____

# 60-DAY
# HOLY SPIRIT
# DEVOTIONAL

## DAY 36

## *There is a Better Way*

*I am telling you this while I am still with
you. But when the Father sends the Spirit of
Holiness, the One like me who sets you free,
he will teach you all things in my name. And
he will inspire you to remember every word
that I've told you.*
*—John 14:25-26 TPT*

There is a better pathway to take in every
situation, and the Spirit of God is leading. He
wants to come in and give us a better way. I
remember Him telling me, "Listen, today while you
are at work, I want you to talk to this person, and I
want you to say it this way." It doesn't always work
out when we don't do things the way God would,
and it gets very frustrating. The Spirit of God is

saying there's a better way, and He's going to give you wisdom and understanding in that.

> *For the Holy Spirit will teach you at that time what needs to be said."*
>
> *—Luke 12:12 NLT*

The Spirit of God wants to speak, and He's going to help you say the words. I remember not even knowing what to say, but He would give me the words to say right at that moment. When it's time to say a word, He will tell you. He will have His way, and He will unveil the truth to you!

**What does God want you to say to someone? Pray about it and yield to the Holy Spirit, and He will give you the words. Go out and share the good news today.**

_____

_____

_____

_____

_____

_____

_____

**DAY 37**

## *The Enforcer of the Blessing*

*We are witnesses of these things, and so is
the Holy Spirit, whom God freely gives to all
who believe in him."
—Acts 5:32 TPT*

He Holy Spirit enforces what God wants to do for you. He has great plans for you, and He wants to fulfill every one of them. Many things can happen during the day to try to stop you from encountering God's blessing. It's almost like you can sense that there are demons who want to impose a curse on you. They want to trip you up and slow you down. They want things to happen that would not benefit you, to hurt you and come against you, but you have the Holy Spirit in you —the enforcer and defender of your faith who wants to bless you. He upholds the New Covenant, and implements what God wants to do, and He is speaking to you saying, "You are healed, you are delivered, and you're going to finish your race." That's what the Holy Spirit is going to do. He's going to encourage you with the truth and say, "You are adopted, and you are accepted in the beloved." These are the things the Holy Spirit wants to speak to you because He's the enforcer of the blessing. Jesus was always blessing people and telling them that they were now free. He wanted them to know the truth. He who the Son sets free is free indeed, and where the spirit of the Lord is, there is freedom (John 8:36, 2 Corinthians 3:17).

*But when the truth-giving Spirit comes, he will unveil the reality of every truth within you. He won't speak on his own, but only what he hears from the Father, and he will reveal prophetically to you what is to come.*
*—John 16:13 TPT*

Meditate on how the Lord has set you free through the Son. The Holy Spirit is there to enforce what God says and does. Let that become known to you in prayer.

_____

_____

_____

_____

_____

_____

_____

_____

_____

_____

_____

_____

_____

_____

_____

_____

_____

_____

# 60-DAY
# HOLY SPIRIT
# DEVOTIONAL

## DAY 38

### *Your Protector*

*But Christ has rescued us from the curse
pronounced by the law. When he was hung
on the cross, he took upon himself the curse
for our wrongdoing. For it is written in the
Scriptures, "Cursed is everyone who is hung
on a tree. "Through Christ Jesus, God has
blessed the Gentiles with the same blessing
he promised to Abraham, so that we who are
believers might receive the promised Holy
Spirit through faith.
—Galatians 3:13-14 NLT*

The Holy Spirit has been assigned to you. He's
your friend, protector, curse breaker, and
advocate to enforce what God says over your life.
When the demonic is working against you, the

Spirit protects you. He is in you and upon you; He covers you.

The Lord has sent the Holy Spirit to enforce the blessings of Abraham on your life. The curse has been placed on Jesus, He hung on a tree, took the curse upon Himself, and you received Abraham's blessing in return. If you encounter the demonic, tell the devils that you are *not* cursed, you are blessed! Break the power of their work against you in Jesus' name.

**Thank the Lord that He gave you the blessing of the Holy Spirit, and that the curse was broken at the cross. Walk in your freedom, and no matter what you face today, remember who the Holy Spirit is to you. Use the power you have within you! Write about your day and how you applied what you learned.**

_____

_____

_____

_____

_____

_____

_____

_____

# 60-DAY
# HOLY SPIRIT
# DEVOTIONAL

**DAY 39**

## *Walking in Truth*

*Let all bitterness, wrath, anger, clamor, and
evil speaking be put away from you, with all
malice. And be kind to one another,
tenderhearted, forgiving one another, even
as God in Christ forgave you.*
*—Ephesians 4:31-32 NKJV*

God wants us to be healthy. He is enforcing
health into our lives. He wants us to allow the
Holy Spirit to come and correct any wrong thinking.
It might be that we need to forgive. If we forgive
and allow the Holy Spirit to correct our thinking, we
can let go of all unforgiveness and receive health.

The Lord is walking us into truth. One of those
truths is healing. When we forgive and let go of

offenses, we become healthy inside. We have to let go of all bitterness and anger if we want to walk in truth.

Sometimes we don't even know what's wrong with us. The Holy Spirit will search your heart and show anything in there that you need to let go of. He's going to give you the mind of the Spirit (Romans 8:27). When you have the mind of the Spirit, you will let go of anything that's not of Him. He's going to help you discern what's hindering you so that you can encounter freedom.

**Ask the Holy Spirit to reveal and highlight those you need to forgive. Ask for forgiveness and release them from judgment. Ask Him to fill your heart with His love and peace towards them. Pray for them and bless them. Allow Him to bring people up throughout the day or week and walk through the above process towards healing. Write about your breakthrough.**

_____

_____

_____

_____

_____

_____

**DAY 40**

## *He Prays the Perfect Will of God*

> *Likewise the Spirit also helps in our weaknesses. For we do not know what we should pray for as we ought, but the Spirit Himself makes intercession for us with groanings which cannot be uttered.*
> *—Romans 8:26*

Can you imagine being able to pray perfect prayers and pray out the perfect will of God? Well, you can, and it will happen to you today if you yield! The Spirit of God wants to help us, not in our strength but our weakness. Whenever you feel weak, it's a perfect opportunity to invite the Holy Spirit into your situation. If you feel lonely, discouraged, or disappointed, ask the Holy Spirit to come in, and He will help you.

He's going to help you to pray out everything the way you should. When you don't know how to pray or what to pray for, the Holy Spirit comes in and helps to super-intercede for you on your behalf. He will make intercession for you with groaning's that cannot be uttered.

**Yield to the Holy Spirit. Let Him speak out of your spirit in other tongues to reveal the perfect will of God. He wants to help you; He is willing.**

_____

_____

_____

_____

_____

_____

_____

_____

_____

_____

_____

_____

_____

# 60-DAY
# HOLY SPIRIT
# DEVOTIONAL

## DAY 41

### *A Move of God*

*When the day of Pentecost came, they were all
together in one place. Suddenly a sound like
the blowing of a violent wind came from
Heaven and filled the whole house where they
were sitting. They saw what seemed to be
tongues of fire that separated and came to rest
on each of them. All of them were filled with
the Holy Spirit and began to speak in other
tongues as the Spirit enabled them.*
*—Acts 2:1-4 NIV*

There is a move of God that is upon this earth
right now, and we can engage in it. The Holy
Spirit is the author of these moves. He's the one
that's moving upon the earth. He starts moving in
people first, and He's moving in you.

I think about what happened in Acts chapter two, where the power of God came on the day of Pentecost. I think about all the things that happened there, how God visited His people just like He said He would. As a believer, God is visiting us daily. You can encounter that move, and you don't have to wait for church. You don't have to wait for certain things to happen because they're already happening inside of you.

**Humble yourself and allow the Spirit of God to intercede and say what the Spirit is saying. Pray in tongues and build yourself up, and then in English as the Spirit gives the interpretation. That humility and brokenness will cause us to move in the Spirit and will cause us to bring in the harvest.**

_____

_____

_____

_____

_____

_____

_____

_____

# 60-DAY
# HOLY SPIRIT
# DEVOTIONAL

**DAY 42**

## *The Comforter*

*Nevertheless I tell you the truth. It is to your
advantage that I go away; for if I do not go
away, the Helper will not come to you; but if
I depart, I will send Him to you.*
—*John 16:7*

The comforter is the Holy Spirit. Jesus described Him as someone who will come and wrap you up to comfort you. You can yield to comfort because the Holy Spirit is that person, and He's inside of you. When you allow God to love on you, you begin to hear His voice. Let the Holy Spirit wrap you up and encourage you.

The Father has already sent the Holy Spirit, and Jesus promised that He'd be with you. He is here with you. The Holy Spirit is the helper, and He is going to bear witness of what Jesus has said. He will remind you of everything that was said. You're going to hear Bible verses come up from within you. You're going to feel the power and the anointing of the Spirit because the comforter is also the power of God.

Did you know that the Holy Spirit rose Jesus from the dead, and that same power is dwelling in you? You have Him right now, and He's going to stay with you until the end of the age. Be encouraged, and let the God of all comfort, comfort you right now through the Holy Spirit.

**Yield to The Holy Spirit in prayer. Ask the Lord to give you scriptures to meditate on. Write them down, and carry them with you. Use them as comfort all day.**

_____

_____

_____

_____

_____

_____

_____

_____

**DAY 43**

## *The Voice of the Holy Spirit*

*When the Spirit of truth comes, he will guide you into all truth. He will not speak on his own but will tell you what he has heard. He will tell you about the future.*
*—John 16:13 NLT*

The voice of the Holy Spirit matches the Word of God. You can attune your sensitivity and recognition of God's voice by reading the Word of God continually. You can listen to His Word through the night. Keep God's Word before you; keep it fresh by reading scripture and spending time with Him. Remind yourself of things that God had said, and do the best you can to place the Word of God before you. Then the voice of the Spirit will match the Word of God.

You can rehearse the voice of God in your spirit by quoting scripture. You will start to hear your voice within, quoting scripture. You can stand by that all day and reinforce it. The Holy Spirit will come forth and speak to you, and it will be the voice of God because it will be scripture. Then when you pray, God will answer you, and He will use His Word to answer you. You'll get to the place where you're going to know the voice of God. The Father is speaking to the Spirit, and the Spirit is speaking to you, and it's going to match the Word.

**Yield to the Holy Spirit and allow Him to bring scripture to you. Make a notecard, and take it with you. Get into a habit, and do this daily. Recite the Word of God throughout the day. Write about your day and how God worked through you using these scriptures.**

_____

_____

_____

_____

_____

_____

_____

# 60-DAY
# HOLY SPIRIT
# DEVOTIONAL

## DAY 44

## *Changing History Through You!*

*For those who are led by the Spirit of God*
*are the children of God.*
*—Romans 8:14 NIV*

D id you know that God can use you in a mighty way wherever you are? You may be in line at the grocery store, begin talking with someone and change history because that person needed to hear what you had to say. The Lord can use you to change their life forever. Even if you never see that person again, they will go forth and they'll have been changed whether they got born again or you gave them an encouraging word that impacted their life, and then that word changes others' lives through them. You are responsible for the changes because you gave the word. You are one of the ones that was used by God to change history. Wherever you go today be mindful that God wants to use you to change history. He is leading and guiding you, and He wants you to be led by the Spirit and speak the truth in love.

**Today in prayer, talk to the Holy Spirit about your day. Ask Him to give you the opportunity to share Him with others. Whether it's a prophetic word or word of knowledge, press in and ask Him to highlight who you are to share the love of God with. He will guide you on what to say. He may show you in prayer as well. Write down how you changed history today.**

_____

_____

_____

_____

_____

_____

_____

_____

_____

_____

# 60-DAY
# HOLY SPIRIT
# DEVOTIONAL

**DAY 45**

## *Jesus' Personality Transforms You*

*And now, because we are united to Christ, we
both have equal and direct access in the realm
of the Holy Spirit to come before the Father!*
*—Ephesians 2:18 TPT*

When I was in Heaven I saw all the purposes
and plans God had for me. He revealed
them to me. I saw that some of them had not been
accomplished, and that I could have done so much
more for Him. I was sent back here and given
another chance.

I want to tell you that you must desire the plans and
purposes God has for you. You have to desire the
fullness of the Spirit. The Holy Spirit wants to show

you the personality of Jesus. Jesus went around doing good, healing everyone that was oppressed of the devil, and that's the plan He has for you as well!

You can go to Him and ask whatever you desire, and it will be given to you. Today, don't ask for just a few things, ask for many things. Jesus said, whatever you desire if you believe that you receive it, you shall have it.

> *"If you believe, you will receive whatever*
> *you ask for in prayer."*
> —*Matthew 21:22 NIV*

**Ask the Holy Spirit to show you the plans He has for you. How is He leading you to help others? How is He transforming you to His likeness? Ask Him for the desires of your heart. Write what He reveals to you.**

_____

_____

_____

_____

_____

_____

_____

## DAY 46

### *The Words the Holy Spirit Speaks*

*"The Holy Spirit is the one who gives life,
that which is of the natural realm is of no
help. The words I speak to you are Spirit
and life. But there are still some of you who
won't believe."*
*— John 6:63 TPT*

The Holy Spirit is the revelation of God. He causes revelation to flow. He gives us the words to speak over our lives and others. The words we speak, are from the other realm and they're sent into this realm. Be mindful that you're taking what is of your Father's and you're transferring it into this realm, whether it is thoughts, revelation, or words.

Let your heart be in tune with the Holy Spirit so that you speak and prophesy over yourself and others. The Father will speak to you to pronounce the things that are not as though they were. He's going to use you to speak from the fire of God and speak life into your world.

**Yield to the Holy Spirit and let Him speak words of life through you. Whatever the Father gives you, release it into this realm. Begin to prophesy over your life and yourself. Prophesy over others as the Lord leads you. Write down what He said.**

_____

_____

_____

_____

_____

_____

_____

_____

_____

_____

_____

_____

**DAY 47**

## *<u>Agreeing with Heaven</u>*

*Remain in me, and I will remain in you. For a branch cannot produce fruit if it is severed from the vine, and you cannot be fruitful unless you remain in me. "Yes, I am the vine; you are the branches. Those who remain in me, and I in them, will produce much fruit. For apart from me you can do nothing.*
*—John 15:4-5 NLT*

The Lord has established certain absolutes in Heaven, but in our lives, in this world, they are conditional. We need to come into agreement with the things of Heaven through the Spirit. Everything that is in the Spirit is absolute, but we must participate in it. We must pray those things which are in Heaven, into this realm being mindful that God has hooked us up with Him and there is an abundant supply. "Thy kingdom come thy will be done on the earth as it is in Heaven" (Matthew 6:10).

The truth of Heaven comes from the vine into the branches, and then it comes through your mouth. Remember that you must participate in these things because they are conditional. In other words, God needs you to agree with Him and participate in His Word. We are the partakers of the divine nature. We are the ones who participate in the Father's will on this earth, and we're going to bring His kingdom into this realm. Today, go out and see that God's will is done. Be a participator and not a spectator.

**Pray and meditate on today's verse. Purpose to remain yielded to the Spirit of God. Come into agreement with what the Spirit wills to do through you. Write what He shows you and step out in it today.**

_____

_____

_____

_____

**DAY 48**

## *Heaven is Coming to the Earth*

*Now all glory to God, who is able, through
his mighty power at work within us, to
accomplish infinitely more than we might
ask or think.
—Ephesians 3:20 NLT*

What is in Heaven is coming to the earth and God is accomplishing it through you. God has many plans and purposes for us in Heaven, but He's placed His Holy Spirit within us. That power that rose Jesus from the dead is in you, and it's surely able to do the mighty things He's written about us in Heaven, it's able to be accomplished in us and through us. It's more than we could ever ask or think. There are no limits with God.

God loves you, and He wants you to abide in Him. He wants you to experience His power on this earth. We're going to come in agreement with Him, and when we do, we will see Him accomplish His purpose in us and in the earth, and He will get the glory for it.

**In prayer today, pray with the limits taken off. He is able to accomplish infinitely anything you ask, so what will you pray for? Whom will you lift up in prayer? The reality is that Heaven is being achieved in and through you. Ask Him to show you. Write about your time in prayer.**

_____

_____

_____

_____

_____

_____

_____

_____

_____

_____

_____

_____

# 60-DAY HOLY SPIRIT DEVOTIONAL

## DAY 49

### *<u>Refuse to Compromise</u>*

*Who Himself bore our sins in His own body
on the tree, that we, having died to sins,
might live for righteousness—by whose
stripes you were healed.
—1 Peter 2:24*

R emaining accountable to the Spirit of Truth
and refusing to compromise your beliefs will
cause you to triumph. There are a lot of situations
we get into where we want to change what we
believe because things don't work out. We can't
apologize for God. We need to believe God for the
impossible, and never back off.

You can't change what you believe just because you
don't see something happening. If it's in the word of

God, you have to stick with it. Be accountable and don't compare yourself to anyone else. Compare yourself to the word of God.

The Lord says you were healed two thousand years ago from the foundations of the world. because that's when Jesus was slain. By His stripes, you *were* healed. Don't compromise your beliefs; receive your healing today. Don't allow the devil or anyone to talk you out of your healing. Stand firm in the will and the word of God, and you'll see everything come to pass.

**In prayer today, thank the Lord for your healing. Thank Him for physical, mental and emotional healing. Thank Him for giving His Son two thousand years ago so you could receive your healing. Let the love of God overwhelm you. Write about it.**

---

---

---

---

---

---

---

---

# 60-DAY
# HOLY SPIRIT
# DEVOTIONAL

**DAY 50**

## *The Spirit of Truth*

*When the Spirit of truth comes, he will guide*
*you into all truth. He will not speak on his*
*own but will tell you what he has heard. He*
*will tell you about the future.*
*—John 16:13 NLT*

S ometimes we need a dose of reality. The Holy
Spirit is the Spirit of Truth, and He's going to
lead you into all Truth. Jesus sent the Spirit of God,
He said He would, and He has! The Holy Spirit is in
you, and He is establishing truth in you. You don't
have to worry about life. He's going to lead you
into life. Life is in God, and life is the Spirit of God.
He's going to speak in you. Even your body is going
to respond to that. You're going to receive healing,
and wisdom today.

When you yield to the Spirit of God, He's going to pray out the will of God. He knows your heart and knows the heart of God. He's going to bring that synchronization within you. Expect that to happen today. Heaven is joining with you. God's will is coming to the earth, and you're going to experience that will. Make sure to encourage others that you encounter today. You're going to receive understanding, and provision today because the Holy Spirit already knows what you need.

**Today in prayer, yield to the Spirit of God. Ask Him to lead you into His Truth and show you about life. He will speak through you and reveal Himself to you. Write what He shows you today in prayer.**

_____

_____

_____

_____

_____

_____

_____

_____

_____

# 60-DAY
# HOLY SPIRIT
# DEVOTIONAL

## DAY 51

## *The Holy Spirit is Aggressive and Bold*

*And when they had prayed, the place where
they were assembled together was shaken;
and they were all filled with the Holy Spirit,
and they spoke the word of God with
boldness.*
*—Acts 4:31*

One of the most important characteristics of the
Holy Spirit is that He is a lot more aggressive
and bolder than we even know. The personality of
the Holy Spirit is revealed here in Acts 4. The place
where they prayed was shaken, and they spoke the
Word of God with boldness.

He is the Spirit that sets you free. There is liberty wherever He is because He is the Spirit of liberty. That Spirit causes you to be bold. You're going to experience this boldness and the place where you pray is going to be shaken!

*Now the Lord is the Spirit; and where the Spirit of the Lord is, there is liberty. But we all, with unveiled face, beholding as in a mirror the glory of the Lord, are being transformed into the same image from glory to glory, just as by the Spirit of the Lord.*
*—2 Corinthians 3:17-18*

**Meditate on today's verse in prayer. Press into the Holy Spirit and agree with Him that you will begin walking in freedom and boldness. What is He speaking to you?**

_____

_____

_____

_____

_____

_____

_____

_____

**DAY 52**

## *A Flash of Your Future*

*For I know the plans I have for you,"*
*declares the Lord, "plans to prosper you*
*and not to harm you, plans to give you hope*
*and a future.*
*—Jeremiah 29:11 NIV*

T he Spirit of God wants to take you and show
you a flash of your future. Can you imagine
the Holy Spirit wants to show you of things to
come? That's what Jesus said, and that is what He
wants to do. The Holy Spirit wants to reveal those
things that you need to know. Jeremiah was shown
by the Spirit of God about Israel's future. God spoke
through him to tell them, "I know the plans I have
for you. I have plans for you to prosper and have a

good and expected end." The Lord had already chosen to bless Israel and have them finish well.

That's the way it is with you. The Lord has His way with you because you submit, and you love Him. You expect Him to intervene in your life. God will give you a flash of your future to show you His plans for you. The Spirit of God wants to encourage you and help you get there. Part of that is giving you a glimpse of the future things to come.

**Ask the Holy Spirit to show you glimpses of your future and thank Him for what's to come. He may show you what needs to break off before reaching that future. It could be mindsets, thoughts, or relationships. As He brings them up, give them to Him and ask Him to show you the way. He will lead you in every step if you'll yield and submit.**

_____

_____

_____

_____

_____

_____

_____

# 60-DAY
# HOLY SPIRIT
# DEVOTIONAL

## DAY 53

## *The Case Against You is Closed*

*So now the case is closed. There remains no accusing voice of condemnation against those who are joined in life-union with Jesus, the Anointed One. For the "law" of the Spirit of life flowing through the anointing of Jesus has liberated us from the "law" of sin and death. For God achieved what the law was unable to accomplish, because the law was limited by the weakness of human nature. Yet God sent us his Son in human form to identify with human weakness. Clothed with humanity, God's Son gave his body to be the sin-offering so that God could once and for all condemn the guilt and power of sin.*
*—Romans 8:1-3 TPT*

The Spirit of God has caused the case against you to be closed because you have been forgiven. He says that there is no condemnation for those who are in Christ Jesus; He wants to confirm that to you today. God has given you the promise of forgiveness. You can live your life completely guilt-free. He has forgiven you and there's no file against you in Heaven.

If you are being reminded of your past, know that He has wiped the past away. Tell the devil that there is no case against you, and no accusing voice against you. The Lord has silenced and taken care of that voice. As you go forth, know that you are a new creature and you've been given a new start in life.

**If you have been hearing and condemnation or the voice of the accuser, remind him that the case has been closed and you are free from the past. Start fresh today and allow yourself to walk in this freedom. Write down some declarations of liberty you can make.**

_____

_____

_____

_____

## DAY 54

### *God's Voice is in You*

*Simply be confident and allow the Spirit of
Wisdom access to your heart, and in that
very moment he will reveal what you are to
say to them.*
—*Luke 12:12 TPT*

G od's voice can be hooked up inside of you. He's in you through the Holy Spirit, and He can hook up with your voice. Your voice and God's voice together make a mighty flow on the earth. When God's voice gets hooked up to your voice, you can speak forth the very oracles of God (1 Peter 4:11). That's why it's important to consciously yield to the Spirit.

Sometimes we don't know what we're going to say, but don't worry about it; you will be given what you're supposed to say at the proper time, by the Holy Spirit.

> *"So when they put you under arrest and hand you over for trial, don't even give one thought about what you will say. Simply speak what the Holy Spirit gives you at that very moment. And realize that it won't be you speaking but the Holy Spirit speaking through you. Brothers will betray each other unto death—even a father his child. Children will rise up to take a stand against their parents and have them put to death. Expect to be hated by all because of your allegiance to my name. But determine to be faithful to the end and you will be saved."*
>
> *—Mark 13:11 TPT*

Be encouraged today that your voice and God's voice are hooked up together inside of you. He's going to give the wisdom and the boldness to speak.

Allow the Holy Spirit to give you God's words today. Declare that you and God are one, and that you only speak what the Father says. Write about your day.

_____

_____

_____

_____

_____

_____

_____

_____

_____

_____

_____

_____

_____

_____

_____

_____

_____

_____

_____

_____

## DAY 55

### *Vibrations in His Voice*

*The voice of the LORD is powerful; the voice*
*of the LORD is majestic. The voice of the*
*LORD splits the mighty cedars; the LORD*
*shatters the cedars of Lebanon.*
*—Psalm 29:4-5 NLT*

When the Holy Spirit speaks, there is a vibration and force that goes out. The authority of God comes through you when you pray in the Spirit and build yourself up in your most Holy of faith. You've synchronized yourself with Heaven, and He comes out of you through your words.

When you speak in tongues, your Spirit gets hooked up with the Most High, and authority and boldness

121

come forth. There is a vibration that goes out and it paralyzes the enemy because your words have power.

Through Jesus Christ, God has given you everything you need for life and godliness in this life. Jesus told us to speak to mountains; we can tell a mountain be removed, and it'll be cast into the sea. He will give you the words to speak that will make hell tremble. Don't hold back; release what the Spirit of God says, and it will cause a vibration in the earth.

**What does the Holy Spirit want to release through you? Make a declaration of it and prophesy the words of the Father.**

_____

_____

_____

_____

_____

_____

_____

_____

_____

# 60-DAY
# HOLY SPIRIT
# DEVOTIONAL

**DAY 56**

## *The Fruit of your Words*

*A man will be satisfied with good by the fruit
of his mouth, And the recompense of a
man's hands will be rendered to him.
—Proverbs 12:14*

When I was with the Lord during my Heavenly visitation, Jesus said to me that each person would be held accountable for every idle word that comes out of their mouth (Matthew 12:36). He taught me about words and to only speak out what I want.

We eat from the fruit of our lips. We eat from our words. When we speak, we're either speaking life or we're speaking death. The book of James talks about our tongue steering our lives and that we need to be speaking words of life (James 3). We need to speak in the direction of where we're going.

We have a rudder, and it's in our mouth. Our tongue is what steers us. We can speak words that will steer our life's direction. Wherever we end up at the end of our life, it's because we steered our life that way with our words. Our tongues are very powerful, and the Lord wants you to choose your words wisely. Start today by declaring where you're going.

**Where are you going? Yield to the Holy Spirit in prayer and talk with Him about the direction you're going with your words. Decide today to speak life and watch the course of your life respond.**

_____

_____

_____

_____

_____

_____

_____

_____

_____

# 60-DAY
# HOLY SPIRIT
# DEVOTIONAL

## DAY 57

## *Speaking to Mountains*

*Listen to the truth I speak to you: Whoever says to this mountain with great faith and does not doubt, 'Mountain, be lifted up and thrown into the midst of the sea,' and believes that what he says will happen, it will be done. This is the reason I urge you to boldly believe for whatever you ask for in prayer—be convinced that you have received it and it will be yours.*
*—Mark 11:23-24 TPT*

There is nothing stopping you from doing what Jesus has told you to do. He said that we can speak to mountains and they will be removed. God would never tell you to do something or go somewhere and then put something in your way to stop you. That's not the way God is and that's not the way He works. Jesus went around doing good

125

and healing everyone who was oppressed of the devil (Acts 10:38). God wasn't making people sick and then telling Jesus to go heal them. God had nothing to do with that sickness. That was the devil. Jesus was working by removing mountains in people's lives and healing them.

He wants you to go around removing mountains and casting them into the sea. You have the same power as Jesus, dwelling in you. The same power that rose Jesus from the dead is quickening your body, your mind, your words, and your thoughts. The Holy Spirit in you gives you the ability to anoint your words and destroy anything that gets in the way of what He's called you to do.

**Today, build yourself up in the most Holy of faith by praying in the Holy Spirit and remaining in the love of God. Be mindful of where you're going. If there is a mountain in your way, tell it to be removed. Write about your day.**

_____

_____

_____

_____

_____

## DAY 58

## *Do not Grieve the Holy Spirit*

*The Holy Spirit of God has sealed you in Jesus*
*Christ until you experience your full salvation.*
*So never grieve the Spirit of God or take for*
*granted his holy influence in your life.*
*—Ephesians 4:30 TPT*

Did you know that the Holy Spirit can be hurt, and that He can be grieved? It's true. That's why we want to be mindful that we do not bring sorrow to the Holy Spirit by how we live. He has identified you as His own and guarantee's that you will be saved on the day of redemption. We need to be careful of what we do and say, not to grieve the Holy Spirit. He's our friend, and He's been sent to be with us forever until the end of the age.

The Holy Spirit has been chosen to go through life with you, and He wants to help you. We're not going to do anything to discourage or hurt Him or cause Him to pull back in any way because we desperately need Him. We need God's breath upon us, and He is our next breath. That breath is the Holy Spirit. May we remain sober minded so that we won't grieve Him in any way.

**Submit to the Holy Spirit in prayer. Put a demand on your authority in Christ. Commit yourself, your actions, and your words as holy unto the Lord and be mindful not to grieve the Holy Spirit. Write about how you overcame and stayed yielded to Him.**

_____

_____

_____

_____

_____

_____

_____

_____

_____

_____

**DAY 59**

## *Don't Put Out the Fire*

*Never restrain or put out the fire of the Holy Spirit.*
*—1 Thessalonians 5:19 TPT*

When you build a fire, you enjoy the heat and light that comes from that fire so much that you don't want anything to diminish that; you want to build it up. Picture yourself fueling the fire of the Holy Spirit, causing it to maintain the bright flame and spread.

I want to see the Holy Spirit spread all over the world. I want the fire of revival and the move of God to go all over the world. I know you do, too. We're not going to do anything to put that fire out.

We're going to do everything we can to build it up and cause it to spread.

You are going on a path and a journey that is taking you to your destiny, and God wants to use you as a minister of fire, as a minister with flames of fire ignited by the fire of God, spreading everywhere (Psalm 104:4). He's giving you everything you need to burn brightly, and you will not in any way diminish or put out the flame of the Holy Spirit.

**Go out and burn brightly. Yield to the Holy Spirit and minister to those the Lord gives you the opportunity. He may give you a word of knowledge or a prophetic word to share with them. Write about your day.**

_____

_____

_____

_____

_____

_____

_____

_____

_____

_____

# 60-DAY
# HOLY SPIRIT
# DEVOTIONAL

## DAY 60

## *Hearing and Seeing in the Spirit*

*For we live by believing and not by seeing.*
*—2 Corinthians 5:7 NLT*

We are not supposed to test the borders or try to find our way blindly. We are already found, and the Holy Spirit is the Spirit of truth. We should be hearing, seeing, and functioning with purpose and destiny. Believing is a form of seeing within our hearts; it is seeing in the Spirit. We receive those things we believe by having the substance of things hoped for. Faith is the substance of things hoped for, the evidence of things not seen, and it's in our heart (Hebrews 11:1).

There is a spiritual sight as well as a physical sight. You may not see anything happening in the physical, but you can see in the spiritual. You can see everything that you believe for.

You can have the evidence and the substance of things hoped for. By faith, you have the ability to see and hear in the Spirit. Faith and hope do not disappoint because you have access to what you are believing for. Take hold of that reality right now. Walk in the Spirit and know that you have spiritual eyesight and spiritual hearing in your heart. Even if it looks contrary in the natural realm, you don't see anything happening, and you haven't received the good news; in your Spirit, you can receive that good news. You may not see what you are believing for in the natural, but that doesn't mean it's not happening in the Spirit!

**Pray in the Spirit and receive spiritual eyesight to see and spiritual ears to hear. The word of God says to believe that you've received it and you shall have it in Jesus' name. Write about what He's imparting to you.**

_____

_____

_____

_____

_____

# Salvation Prayer

*Lord God,*
*I confess that I am a sinner.*
*I confess that I need Your Son, Jesus.*
*Please forgive me in His name.*
*Lord Jesus, I believe You died for me and that*
*You are alive and listening to me now.*
*I now turn from my sins and welcome You into my heart.*
*Come and take control of my life.*
*Make me the kind of person You want me to be.*
*Now, fill me with Your Holy Spirit, who will show me*
*how to live for You. I acknowledge You before men as*
*my Savior and my Lord. In Jesus's name. Amen.*

If you prayed this prayer, please contact us at info@kevinzadai.com for more information and materials.

We welcome you to join our network at Warriornotes.tv for access to exclusive programming.

To enroll in our ministry school, go to: www.Warriornotesschool.com.

**Visit KevinZadai.com for additional ministry materials.**

# About Dr. Kevin L. Zadai

Kevin Zadai, ThD, was called to the ministry at the age of ten. He attended Central Bible College in Springfield, Missouri, where he received a Bachelor of Arts in theology. Later, he received training in missions at Rhema Bible College and a ThD at Primus University. He is currently ordained through Rev. Dr. Jesse and Rev. Dr. Cathy Duplantis.

At the age of thirty-one, during a routine day surgery, he found himself "on the other side of the veil" with Jesus. For forty-five minutes, the Master revealed spiritual truths before returning him to his body and assigning him to a supernatural ministry.

Kevin holds a commercial pilot's license and is retired from Southwest Airlines after twenty-nine years as a flight attendant. Kevin is the founder and president of Warrior Notes School of Ministry. He and his lovely wife, Kathi, reside in New Orleans, Louisiana.

# Other Books and Study Guides by Dr. Kevin L. Zadai

*Kevin has written over fifty books and study guides Please see our website at www.Kevinzadai.com for a complete list of materials!*

*60-Day Healing Devotional*

*60-Day Devotional: Encountering the Heavenly Sapphire1*

*60-Day Devotional: Supernatural Finances*

*The Agenda of Angels*

*The Agenda of Angels Study Guide*

*A Meeting Place with God, The Heavenly Encounters Series Volume*

*Days of Heaven on Earth*

*Days of Heaven on Earth: A Study Guide to the Days Ahead Days of Heaven on Earth Prayer and Confession Guide*

*Encountering God's Normal*

*Encountering God's Normal: Study Guide Encountering God's Will*

*Encountering the Heavenly Sapphire Study Guide*

*From Breakthrough to Overthrow: Study Guide*

*Have you Been to
the Altar Lately?*

*Heavenly Visitation*

*Heavenly Visitation:
Study Guide*

*Heavenly Visitation
Prayer and Confession
Guide*

*How to Minister to the
Sick: Study Guide*

*It's Rigged in Your
Favor*

*It's all Rigged in Your
Favor: Study Guide*

*It's Time to Take Back
Our Country*

*Lord Help Me to
Understand Myself:
Study Guide*

*Mystery of the
Power Words*

*Mystery of the
Power Words:
Study Guide*

*The Notes of a Warrior:
The Secrets of Spiritual
Warfare Volume 1
Study Guide*

*The Notes of a Warrior:
The Secrets of Spiritual
Warfare Volume 2
Study Guide*

*The Power of Creative
Worship: Study Guide*

*Prayer Nations With
Kevin & Kathi Zadai*

*Praying from the
Heavenly Realms*

*Praying from the
Heavenly Realms:
Study Guide*

*Receiving from Heaven*

*Receiving from Heaven:
Study Guide*

5

Made in the USA
Middletown, DE
12 March 2022

62478629R00086